TO FUR, WITH LOVE

5/1/2018

Millers —

Nice to meet you!

TO FUR, WITH LOVE

America's Oldest Furrier

Richard L. Swartz

Cover photo courtesy of Azzurra Piccardi, Samantha De Reviziis fur influencer Lady Fur

© 2016 Richard L. Swartz
All rights reserved.

ISBN-13: 9781523803798
ISBN-10: 1523803797
Library of Congress Control Number: 2016903872
Createspace Independent Publishing Platform
North Charleston, South Carolina

Author's Preface

In your hands are the proverbial bank address, vault combination, safe deposit box number and key, and the materials therein—stock certificates, passports, foreign currencies, gold bars, and other sundry precious metals, diamonds (sealed within a faded business envelope), black-and-white photographs, credit cards, and family heirlooms…*everything*!

In your hands is every secret I know about luxury goods.

No matter how reasonable or reserved, any purveyor of said goods who happened across this book would want to burn it, but that would be impossible because no flame can incinerate these virtual pages. He or she would rather delete this content and set the web afire with terror than to ever have you discover what I know about this very secretive order.

Why, then, should I divulge these secrets? Or, you may ask, to paraphrase a line from the film adaptation of *The Godfather*, where Marlon Brando had surrendered his mind and body to method acting, "Why do you come to me? Why do I deserve this generosity?"

My answer is simple: as the representative of the fourth generation of the Swartz bloodline and as the president of Mano Swartz Furs, I refuse to be a bystander to the cheapening of language, to the inflated use of the word *luxury*, and to the mistaken belief that the more expensive something is, the more superior that item will be.

I refuse to silently abet the unraveling of standards and traditions—to sign my own death warrant. Instead, I am issuing this statement. I will not be any part of a moral crime that denies consumers value but demands more and more of their dollars.

I will not discard over a century of family history and craftsmanship, of loyalty from my extended family of customers and workers, and of fealty to my hometown of Baltimore, Maryland, for the indulgence of lust, gluttony, greed, sloth, wrath, envy, or pride.

I will not destroy the legacy of my father and his father and his father's father, my paternal great-grandfather, Mano Swartz.

After the fury of two world wars; the Great Depression; international upheaval and domestic strife; religious persecution abroad, with its inferno of Nazi hatred; and racial apartheid at home, with its ferocious fire hoses, gangs, and police violence, I know too much. And I have seen too much to simply squander the achievements of the men and women I love.

This book is not, therefore, just about how to buy and care for the right fur coat. Rather, it is an all-purpose guide to purchasing the right luxury goods.

Richard Swartz

Introduction

My story is a family-business story. It's about how a young man came to America and built a luxury retail business that continues to impact lives over a century later.

It is a story of survival and thriving in the face of adversity. A journey that spans centuries and continents while holding social justice as a core value.

And yes, it is a story about fur, one of nature's greatest gifts.

1

The Legend: One Man's Epic Pursuit of Excellence

I am the great-grandson of Mano Swartz, founder of Mano Swartz Furs (established in 1889), America's oldest furrier.

The story of this company begins with a transatlantic voyage, a two-week tutorial in American history narrated by an old Union soldier speaking to a young boy from Mitteleuropa.

Mano Swartz, founder of Mano Swartz Furs

The veteran befriends the child because of the boy's ability to speak German and thus to convert the guttural pronouncements about departure and arrival times—*their* departure time, via steamship—into intelligible English. And he teaches the young Mano Swartz about a country torn asunder by every drop of blood drawn with the lash and repaid by another drawn with the sword; and then, in an attempt to bind up the nation's wounds, in this reconciliation between those devoted altogether to *saving* the Union without war and those insurgent agents seeking to *destroy* it by making war, the president of the United States, a man with the devotion of Abraham and the vision of Moses, is felled by an assassin's bullet before he can cherish a just and lasting peace among his fellow citizens and with all nations.

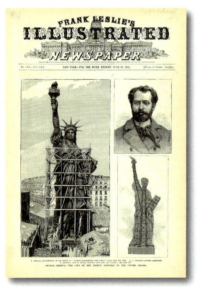

I picture my great-grandfather on that boat, a five-dollar silver certificate bearing the portrait of Ulysses S. Grant in his pocket, a gratuity for ensuring that the veteran made it aboard the ship, and I try to imagine their entry into the Port of New York. The Statue of Liberty would have been under construction, covered in scaffolding and catwalks, a copper-colored goddess free of the ravages of oxidation, smoke, pollution, and neglect, a little over a mile from Manhattan and the island's soot-covered tenements and neo-Gothic spires.

His New York, with its blend of fellow Eastern European Jews and Yiddish speakers, a stratified island of Knickerbocker wealth and Dutch ancestry, was not separated by fences, though there are images aplenty of Fifth Avenue mansions with iron bars and ornate finials. Instead, it was enclosed by invisible walls of class and power—from the temples of finance and the House of Morgan to internecine warfare among the poor for patronage jobs and the stabbings among Irish gangs. Mano Swartz entered a city of tribes, toil, tears, vengeance, and graft.

What, you may ask, does this detour into genealogy have to do with buying and learning how to maintain the quality of a fur coat? In a word: everything!

If you do not know the story of a luxury brand, if you are unable to explain the values a company represents, then you will not get value for your money.

For there is a difference between something that is expensive *relative to other things* and something that is a rip-off plain and simple.

Few travelers would argue, for example, that the Four Seasons Hotels Inc. is a magnet for cheapskates and misers. They would be much more likely to describe the hotels as destinations for magnates and munificent guests who value the service, comfort, design, dining, use of native architecture, and respect for local customs. This is what makes the company's properties throughout North America, Central and South America, Europe, the Middle East and Africa, and Asia and the Pacific so distinctive.

Not for nothing does the website for the Four Seasons have a page about "Extraordinary Experiences," where vacationers can consider embarking on a "Golden Triangle Sunrise Elephant Trek." The trek itself includes a preparatory session where travelers learn about using vocal commands to mount and dismount from these gentle giants before riding their own elephants and watching the sun rise over the Mekong Delta. This is the first of many adventures in Thailand's Golden Triangle.

I am a fan of the brand, which is why I cite the company's emphasis on experiences—the performances that make you feel like a viceroy in an imaginary province belonging to Her Majesty's Government, or a naturalist walking through waist-high amber waves of grain. The details of each encounter seem so real that participants can easily imagine life in a former Florentine convent, even after it has been recommissioned as a Tuscan hotel (decorated with various pieces of Renaissance art and antiquities, as well as original frescoes and fountains).

That is the magic of life in a hotel. Hotels appeal to adults and children, albeit for different reasons. They appeal because they are the domain of Vladimir Nabokov, of Eloise. One roams the Plaza Hotel in Midtown Manhattan, remembering Eloise's story as it was immortalized in a series of books. And Nabokov's spirit infuses the halls of the Montreux Palace with the novels and wordplay of a master prose stylist.

There Nabokov sat on the terrace with his wife, Vera, facing the shores of Lake Léman (Lake Geneva), having an al fresco breakfast of tea, fruit, and toast. Nabokov was a White Russian, an exile of Bolshevism and Nazism, his brother a victim (prisoner number 28631) of Hitler's archipelago of detention and death. And the writer's silhouette continues to inspire and intimidate us across the veil of years.

From these experiences, the suite of a luxury hotel is a room alive with history. So, too, are the note cards containing the correspondence, thoughts, and observations of Mano Swartz.

Those cards and letters are the miscellany of an observer of Europe's convulsive (and soon-to-collapse) empires and the rise of American power. The sheaves of papers, yellowed by age and as short lived as the episodes they chronicle, now exist in digital files. An icon enlarges the print, zooming in and fading out, as I scroll from top to bottom—and as I record the transition from the end of one century to the beginning of another, from the founding of Mano Swartz Furs to the armistice with Germany. I, unlike my great-grandfather, know what events that young man will see, what pleas (from desperate relatives) he will receive, and what dreadful rumors (later substantiated) he will hear.

Mano Swartz Furs, downtown Baltimore, Maryland

I present the story of that man because his humanity infuses my office with the spirit of love and loss, with the brightness of the morning and the darkness of mourning, and with the euphoria of success and the struggle for survival that is life itself.

I know how his story ends, yet I work to ensure that his name is eternal. That story is my inheritance—I am its custodian, not its owner. The difference between the two is stark, because it is one person's responsibility—it is this writer's duty—to perpetuate family customs while avoiding the temptations of the quick buck, the sellout, and the worship of mammon.

Mano Swartz, 1864–1941   James Swartz, 1896–1977   Mano Swartz II, 1922–2009

To go after a quick buck would be a betrayal of everything Mano Swartz is. If I did so, I would be unable to look at the portrait of my great-grandfather and the one of his son and of his son's son, my father, each one a reward for a minimum of forty years of work. The paintings are a sequential alignment of over a century of history. Three of them hang in my office, and if I betrayed our values, I would have them removed from the wall, exposing pale spaces of dustlike ashes that would symbolize my indifference toward the events each man represents.

Gone would be the battle for civil rights, a struggle for the ages (and a pursuit that will last the ages), were I to forget my grandfather's refusal to accept the terms and conditions of a manifesto of hate, enforced by silence and policed by threats and violence.

Gone would be a history of private heroism, advertised to no one but known by everyone: that Mano Swartz Furs would not maintain the color line, that the company would not be an accomplice to a moral crime with a legal mask, that it would not run a segregated or exclusionary business where blacks could not work or shop with whites.

Selma, Alabama, 1965

Baltimore, Maryland, 2015

What does it matter to today's consumer, more than a half century after the passage of the Civil Rights Act of 1964 and the Voting Rights Act of 1965, after the crucible of Birmingham and Memphis, after the assassination of a King, and after the election of the son of a Kansan and a Kenyan, that my grandfather decided not to go along just so his business could get along?

The answer is this: a company cannot preserve its standards—it will not have any standards of decency and respect—if it has no soul.

My grandfather's actions prove that a company is more than the law's strict definition of personhood.

His decision, despite the small number of black customers who could afford to buy a fur coat from Mano Swartz Furs, was not then—and it is not now—a symbolic gesture. I remember the phone calls at the office and at our home at all hours of the day and night from cowards promising to attack or kill that "dirty Jew," my grandfather, for his love of a "mongrel race."

I remember the worry among my family and our extended family of workers and friends that the company would close, that there would not be enough customers—that there would not be fifty righteous people, or forty-five or forty or thirty or twenty, not even ten—to defend an issue as old as the scriptures and as clear as the American Constitution.

I also recall a more private but no less dangerous battle at home for a cause that still rages abroad. It is an issue that ends every Passover Seder with a promise that is also a pledge—a sacred covenant to those Zionist pioneers, my paternal grandfather among them—to make real the words "Next year in Jerusalem."

It is an oath to the victims of that monstrous inferno of smoke that issued from locomotives transformed into funeral trains and from the chimneys of the crematoria at Auschwitz, Buchenwald, Belzec, Dachau, Mauthausen, and Gusen.

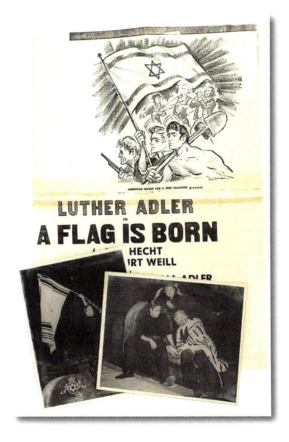

In the aftermath of that catastrophe—the commission of a crime without a name—I have within my desk drawer the letterhead and typography, the summons to duty, for a noble campaign: *The American League for a Free Palestine* (ALFP). It bears the dateline August 7, 1947, and the group announces its forthcoming meeting, to be held on Tuesday (August 12, 1947) at 8:30 p.m. at 909 North Charles Street, in Baltimore, Maryland.

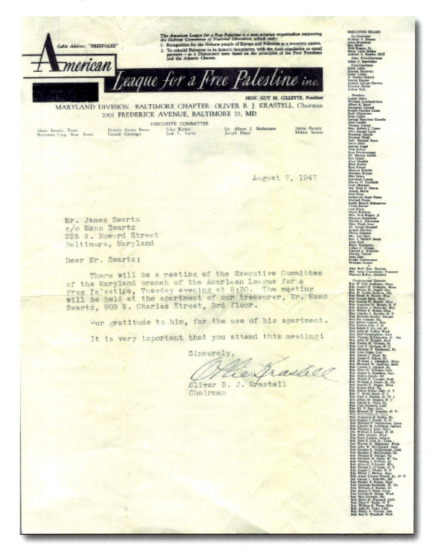

That is the last page of the first chapter of our modern Genesis—not our Exodus—involving the birth of the Jewish State of Israel.

That is a story of Hebrew redemption and a tale of righteous bravery among the Gentiles of the nations.

We owe it to the saviors of our people to give them life in the Holy Land by planting trees and creating one vast canopy of greenery in a forest where the seeds from the Old World grow in the soil—and soul—of the New. And so we have, and so we continue to do.

I cannot help but think of my grandfather's fidelity to justice, how zealous he was in his quest to aid an underground army with the money and material necessary to expel the forces of the British Empire and repel the invading armies of Egypt, Jordan, Iraq, Syria, and Lebanon.

I cannot help but think of my grandfather's patriotism as an American and his position among the patriarchs of a chosen people, not a better race or a superior collection of the Almighty's disciples, but a people in a seemingly never-ending tale of enslavement and emancipation, of stubborn pride and swift consequences from above, and of sundered garments against God—a protest throughout the long and lamentable rise of Hitler—and tributes to the very same creator of the universe who blesses Israel with much more than milk and honey. My grandfather decided to answer this call, that he would defy the odds and the opponents, that he would persist—if necessary for years and if necessary alone—until a people without a land would accept a sliver of territory, in peace, rather than lose everything because of the uncertainty of war.

And yet the winds of war were to envelop Jaffa and Jerusalem, and Bethlehem and Beersheba, and the mountains of Galilee and the Golan Heights.

They were to sweep through the White House and the State Department, eliciting favor from the former and fury from the latter, pitting a man of military stature against a haberdasher outfitted with a presidential wardrobe and the perquisites of his awesome predecessor, Franklin Delano Roosevelt.

The voice of James Swartz echoes from one century to another, from the decimation of a divided Germany to the playing of "Hatikvah" (the

Israeli national anthem) and the entry of refugees into a country that chooses to be a light among the nations; "Yerushalayim Shel Zahav."

My grandfather's life is the answer to that call.

❖ ❖ ❖

Today, the calls come from consumers of all races and religions and of all interests and places. There are African American buyers, including athletes and entertainers, as well as one who is so rich, so famous, and so successful (in TV and film, behind or in front of a microphone) that her last name is excessive; she just is…Oprah!

Oprah!

MANO SWARTZ FUR CUSTOMERS

The calls come from designers and patrons from around the world, and the calls come from residents throughout the city and suburbs of my beloved Baltimore.

By answering their calls, I answer the call—and I defend the honor—of the great men and women, some of them known only to my great-grandfather, whose letters for help, with their coded messages (to confound the Nazis), contain pleas for assistance and warnings about Europe's descent into madness at the hands of Hitler and Stalin.

When I imagine my great-grandfather reading those letters as an American citizen on American soil and recalling his final visit to Europe as a witness to (and within earshot of) the assassination of Archduke Franz Ferdinand, I like to think that I know how his conscience would respond to any plea for justice and compassion.

Indeed, I know how the conscience of *his* company, which is *my* company, would react to injustice somewhere. The company would react by preventing its spread everywhere.

Those values are the lifeblood of this company, and they have earned it a reputation for excellence.

Find the essence of a brand, such as its story and its virtues, and you will have a product worth owning.

2

The Secret: Inside the World of Luxury Goods

When you enter a realm of pure imagination, it must be real…and extraordinary. It must be as whimsical and authentic as the dreams of a luxury brand's namesake or protector.

It must be, for each first-time visitor, breathtaking in such a way that its realness—from the scents and sounds to the feelings of touch and taste—transfixes us in a moment of sensory overload.

Such is the world of a fictional confectioner, and such is the world of actual men like Walt Disney and Ralph Lauren.

The confectioner revives our innocence with the commodity every child covets. Even if rolls of licorice, rivers of chocolate, gardens of gumdrops, or pockets of whipped cream fill a massive room in a gigantic factory, boys and girls can never get enough of this thing: candy!

There is candy of every color and stripe, of every size and shape, so delicious and plentiful that it is, in that place (and only that place), nutritious. Everything is edible, and nothing is impossible because, in a world of pure imagination, there are no laws but one: happiness.

So there is a glass elevator that can move in every direction—just press a button, and go (up, up, and away)—and that can accelerate through a panel of skylights. Segueing from smashing through the roof's exterior to singing a soothing melody, the man-child—*that* genius—with the purple top hat and velvet frock, the satin bow tie and the violet lamé vest, embraces you while you fly heavenward.

Such is the world of pure imagination.

Such is the world of a great story, and such is the world (of a different but no less creative tale) of the two men referenced above, Walt Disney and Ralph Lauren.

Store　　　　　Showroom　　　　Current Staff　　　　1973 Staff

So, too, is our showroom: a collection of offices, fitting rooms, and photographic displays of styles past and present, where we work as a family, united in spirit and joined together in words and deeds, to achieve excellence.

This is our home, and here the "Mano Swartz Experience" thrives amid splendor and solidarity. Our staff, present and past, have executed this mission—and it's a critical mission. Without them, the Mano Experience would never have been a reality that touched so many.

Not for nothing does the fashion industry speak of houses of style, such as the House of Chanel, the House of Armani, and the House of Dior. Each namesake is a house (or a granite townhouse) in a literal sense, with walkways, stone balusters and sweeping staircases, marble fireplaces, and leaded lights in sitting rooms and dining rooms. These houses also have converted service kitchens where models and designers come and go, clients schedule fittings, and tailors cut and sew.

If you want to ensure a luxury brand is worthy of your investment, use this chapter as your guide.

Remind yourself that a luxury brand has an office (or offices)—not cheap furniture, cubicles, and a time clock. Put another way, if a brand aspires to greatness, it does not reduce itself to shame and embarrassment.

There cannot be any separation between perception and reality.

Take, for instance, Walt Disney's private apartment (above the Main Street Firehouse) at Disneyland in Anaheim, California.

The apartment, preserved to maintain its original appearance, is a five-hundred-square-foot manifestation of Disney's personality; it's a Middle American time capsule, with an Edison phonograph, a Regina music box, a Victorian-style telephone, and a covered (with vines) patio, replete with white wicker furniture and an interior decorated with rose-patterned carpeting, cranberry-colored drapes, and various ceramics.

This hideaway, decorated by a set designer for many Disney films, has all the qualities of verisimilitude—it *seems* real—without the messiness of everyday life.

The apartment recalls the nearby sights and sounds of a small-town railroad station, its plumes of smoke and the pitch of a train whistle marking the course of a mighty engine of industry and adventure making its way across Missouri and Colorado, Utah and Nevada, to the fragrant air of California and the Pacific Ocean.

The apartment is both a point of passing and an end point because, all appearances to the contrary, the air of former citrus fields—the orange groves of Orange County, California—perfumes the atmosphere of this self-enclosed frontier and its Mark Twain Riverboat attraction; there is a succulent scent to the Rivers of America and New Orleans Square that takes visitors from a century of locomotives and steamboats to the rocketry of the Space Age and a Mission to Mars.

From the entrance of the Sleeping Beauty Castle to the electric hum of the Disneyland Monorail System, the place and the product are the same for workers and customers alike.

If, after this virtual smorgasbord of candy, locomotion, time travel, and flight, you choose to ask, "What does a company's office, or Walt Disney's old apartment, have to do with the world of luxury goods?" I say, "Let us take a journey to New York City."

A side note: while there are many American cities, there is only one "City," which has been reimagined as Gotham and Metropolis for a reason.

Batman is not the Dark Knight of Boston or Philadelphia. He does not answer a distress signal from a modified klieg searchlight that pierces the sky over Cleveland.

And Clark Kent writes for a great metropolitan newspaper. His migration does not take him from the prairies and cornfields of Kansas to a typewriter six paces from a window with a view of downtown Buffalo.

The City is an island of costumes, of Yankee pinstripes and Wall Street power ties, of Broadway conductors and subway conductors, of Central Park poets and Park Avenue patrons; it is the City of the Caped Crusader and the Man of Steel.

No one makes as many costumes—and wears so many himself—as Ralph Lauren.

He is a rancher and a cowboy; a movie mogul and a leading man; an honorary Episcopalian and a proud Jew; a neighbor of James Bond (rather, the owner of a home in Jamaica where Ian Fleming, the creator of 007, had a nearby estate named Goldeneye); and the father-in-law of Lauren Bush, the granddaughter of George Herbert Walker Bush and the niece of George Walker Bush.

He is the American Dream, outfitted with a sweater that bears the American flag.

If you doubt the power of his costumes, consider this taped birthday tribute from Woody Allen to Ralph Lauren:

"Ralph always thought he could be an actor," said Allen. "We had lunch one day, and he said, 'Put me in a picture.'

"I said, 'Who do you see yourself as?'

"He said, 'Steve McQueen, Gary Cooper.'

"I said, 'Ralph, you're a short little Jew.'

"He said, 'Not when I'm dressed.'"

A brief digression: Ralph Lauren is a longtime admirer of Cary Grant, with whom he became a good friend, and for whom Warren Beatty tried to recruit to play the lead (a role Beatty assumed after Grant—and Muhammad Ali—turned him down) in *Heaven Can Wait*.

In the film, Beatty's character, Joe Pendleton, is the late fictional quarterback of the Los Angeles Rams.

Taken before his time, and unable to return to his body because it was cremated, Pendleton inhabits the body of Leo Farnsworth...and buys the Rams and installs himself as quarterback prior to the team's entry into the Super Bowl against the Pittsburgh Steelers.

It's improbable, yes, but very entertaining nonetheless, because one of Farnsworth's quirks, aside from owning an NFL franchise, involves playing dress-up.

When Pendleton first becomes Farnsworth, his butler says, "Your helmet, sir. Your polo helmet, sir."

Farnsworth responds, "Thanks. Do I play polo?"

And the butler says, "Not really, sir."

Perhaps a handful of people play polo; it is, after all, known as the sport of kings. But millions of consumers own shirts with a branded collar label, and on the reverse side of that label is a thread alignment that is difficult to copy, bearing the word *Polo* (in a white rectangle with a blue background), followed by the words (below the rectangle) *by Ralph Lauren*.

Lauren is a perfect summation of this chapter because you cannot create something great if you do not surround yourself with greatness.

You must *become* a character.

Ralph Lauren *is* that character when he says, "I'm Batman...I've been Batman for a long time, so people give me Batman gifts."

Or, to quote Cary Grant, "Everyone wants to be Cary Grant. Even I want to be Cary Grant. I pretended to be somebody I wanted to be until finally I became that person."

3

What You Need to Know Before You Buy a Luxury Good

Now that we know what a luxury retailer owes you, we must understand how that same retailer should treat you.

All of *that*—the promotional grandeur, the light shows, the magic, and the feats of derring-do announced by an impresario of charm and theatricality—is revealed as an illusion after one enters the seemingly real fiefdom of wealth (or "old money"), absolute comfort, and manufactured innocence.

It is a beautiful illusion, but it's an illusion just the same.

The performance is obligatory but never labored: it should look and feel authentic, like you are, in fact, the center of this self-enclosed universe of cashmere, cotton, wool, mahogany, mink, sable, and sumptuous swatches of leather, silk, and satin.

Once a salesperson approaches you, the spell is over. That is *not* a bad thing because how that man or woman behaves will determine whether the performance continues (albeit in a different and more participatory fashion), or whether you make a run for the exit.

It is easier to know when to leave and to do so with great speed because the proverbial "tells" are so obvious: the pressure to buy, and to buy *right now*, is something you should never experience while browsing in a high-end boutique or department store.

If a salesperson sees you focus on or examine (by sorting through a shelf of color-coordinated items) a specific coat or sweater, and he says,

"We have one left in stock. I can save it for you, as a favor, until tomorrow morning. I cannot guarantee it will be available after we open at ten," that unexpected—and even startling, which is why the salesperson says it—statement can make you jump, falter, or stutter. It should also make you bid farewell to the salesperson and the store.

The intrusive manner and the high-pressure sales tactics described above prove at least two things.

First, that salesperson has a weekly or monthly sales quota he must meet.

Second, whether the aggressive employee has a quota or is just an overzealous anomaly, by seeking to move inventory, to earn consistently large commissions, and to rapidly advance within a company, his or her actions belie the very purpose of that store's existence. The luxury retail environment is a sacred space; it is *not* a training ground for used-car salesmen or disreputable individuals "managed" by some belligerent but invisible (to the consumer) boss who uses fear and intimidation to mislead shoppers and induce buyer's remorse.

All of this reveals another "tell" about that retailer—namely, the goods and services within that store are *not* worthy of the designation of luxury.

The reason this hypothetical brand is not a maker of luxury products is simple: craftsmanship speaks for itself.

A premium item is so identifiable—the sophistication of a Rolls-Royce Phantom, which has a manufacturer's suggested retail price of $482,275, is so apparent—that a salesperson does not, first and foremost, try to sell you anything.

He or she is there to provide you with an experience that reflects the brand.

What, then, is the role of a salesperson on behalf of a luxury retailer?

It is to provide an uplifting, ephemeral experience and to help you come to the best possible conclusion. Sometimes this may mean suggesting that you not buy.

Once, a very important judge came to our store to trade in his granddaughter's coat because he felt it was out of style. Upon examination I felt it was truly classic and still had years of wear. I told him that, and he was so shocked and happy to know what the real deal was.

The luxury experience has to take us away from ourselves and our daily emotional pain, away from our stresses and worries. When buying a fur for a loved one (even if that loved one is yourself), the time buying must be more than the sum of its parts. There must be a true human interaction as the buyer and seller meet on a deep level of understanding.

"Welcome to Mano Swartz."

Those four words, enunciated clearly and invitingly, should put the customer's mind at ease. Your Mano Experience is about to begin.

Before he has a chance to say those four words, he will have said much more.

And of course we are there to serve you, not to pressure, cajole, or induce you to spend more money.

I conclude this section with two words: social justice.

If you want to know what true grit is, let me tell you about Paul. Paul was a man I met in front of our store in downtown Baltimore in 1973 when I was fourteen years old. My grandfather was the only merchant who allowed Paul to stay all day in front of our store. The others felt he scared away customers.

Too proud to accept or elicit pity and a model of charity when seeking the same from others, Paul was a living parable—a man whose presence was a test of the essence of our character.

A double amputee whose legs had been severed in a car crash, Paul had a legacy that was like a secular version of that of his biblical namesake. On a journey through the economic desert of the ghetto, two feet above the very earth he would have been six feet under, propelled by brushes swept by the sinews of his arms, Paul, through his presence outside our store, reminded us that no man—no beggar or vagrant—is not a man.

His example still inspires me.

That principle finds its home in our house, where a gentle warrior—merciless in the boxing ring and mellow outside it—can walk into Mano Swartz Furs fresh from one of his many daily workouts and feel like the champion he is.

That professional fighter, the owner of *many* of our coats, caps, scarves, jackets, vests, and gloves, is Willie "For Real" Williams, Baltimore's own light-heavyweight boxer, whose ability to stick and move—to jab his way through hardship and defend himself against opponents who would bankrupt our city and corrupt a famed sport—is impressive, indeed.

In so many words, Willie is for real—and so is Mano Swartz Furs.

We know how difficult things can be, which is why we make our service as personal as it should be, as soothing as it must be, as comforting as it is now and shall always be.

You are always welcome, whether you buy ten furs or browse among twenty but purchase none.

Our home is yours.

4

Enjoying Your Fur Coat: A Lifestyle Choice, Not a Museum Piece

You are, for the purposes of this chapter (and on behalf of every reader with an interest in buying the right luxury good), a valued customer—you are a member of the Mano Swartz family.

As this video; https://www.youtube.com/watch?v=-HT7YL8Hg1 explains, and as the clips on our official site demonstrate, there are seven factors that should influence your purchase of a fur coat: color, style, lifestyle, length, quality, fit, and price.

Notice that these elements are *personal* variables: taken individually or reviewed collectively, these seven rules define what you want—and symbolize the very best we have to offer. Your experience will be enhanced by the quality of the material and by the peace of mind that comes from learning that this product is not only an investment by you—it is also a commitment by us for you.

That fact comes with its own Mano Swartz "Certificate of Appraisal," an official record that communicates the replacement value of your fur coat or related garments purchased from America's oldest furrier.

Consider this certificate to be an additional statement of financial and ethical significance, since it is a living document—one that reflects current price trends—and has behind it the full faith and credit we possess and the expertise and integrity we represent. It projects the accurate economic cost (the emotional value is incalculable) for an insurer to pay for a replacement fur.

FUR INSURANCE APPRAISAL

March 30, 2016

DESCRIPTION			APPRAISED VALUE
Natural Sable Coat Origin: Russia	Length: 54"	Sweep: 100"	$ 100,000.00

Mano Swartz Inc.

By: *[signature]*

Richard Swartz President
4th Generation Furrier

The appraisal of the aforesaid fur garment is given upon the express condition that it is not to be considered a representation on the part of Mano Swartz Inc. to purchase (or accept as a trade-in) said article at the appraised insurance value, nor is it to be construed as an offer to purchase at said price at any time, nor is it a guarantee that said article will realize the appraised amount at any public, private or other sale. The appraisal for the above fur garment is based on the estimated actual market conditions now latent existing on the date of the appraisal and is made for insurance purposes only, to reflect the replacement value on this date.

10801 Falls Road, Lutherville, MD 21093 | 410-825-9000 | www.manoswartz.com

Remember, too, that our name is on the line. From the end of one century to the birth and conclusion of the most convulsive century on record to the end of the first half of the second decade of the twenty-first century, a Mano Swartz fur has been a totem of love, an heirloom of passion, and a restyled piece of fashion history.

Furs are the natural choice, because when choosing fur, you are buying from a trade that is highly regulated and sustainable. Furs are the best environmental choice one can make. The carbon footprint is miniscule; the fur itself is reusable, recyclable, and biodegradable.

For the latest on the fur trade, follow Lady Fur, http://www.welovefur.com/, the world's most important fur blogger.

Photo: Azzurra Piccardi Samantha De Reviziis fur influencer Lady Fur

MAINTENANCE THROUGH SUMMER STORAGE: GLORY THROUGH GLAZING

If you want to cherish your fur and wear it with delight, you need to have us store and condition your fur each April.

We will eliminate the airborne pollutants, the accumulated debris of dust and cosmetics, and the residue of perfumes and fragrances that can exhaust the natural oils in the leather underneath your fur coat or fur accessory.

We will isolate these agents, including the residue of hairspray and any other alcohol-based products that can weaken the shine, shape, suppleness, and longevity of your fur.

Our proprietary conditioning preserves that glorious glaze and keeps your fur looking like the beauty it is.

This process, honed, refined, and perpetuated over the course of more than 125 years, is a customized exercise—for a personalized product—that includes having a veteran inspector examine the fur with the meticulous eye of a collector and the sensitive feeling of an artist.

STAYING IN STYLE BY RESTYLING: A BELOVED FUR MADE NEW AGAIN

A Mano Swartz fur is never the prisoner of a time because it is always current with the times.

In so many words, fur restyling, a "Mano Makeover," as this video; https://www.youtube.com/watch?v=MfwkODWCXGc reveals is a way to always have your fur in style.

Our credit is in the creation of furs and their transformation into luxury goods that are beloved among families and bequeathed to daughters, granddaughters, sisters, and friends; they are furs to wear with pride, enjoying the warmth of the garment and the goodwill of our heart.

Our name is our legacy.

OF MEN AND BOOKS
Quotations From Famous Authors

Compiled by
MANO SWARTZ

TOGETHER WITH A PORTRAIT OF MANO SWARTZ,
A PAINTING BY D. W. STOKES, A FOREWORD BY LEONARD
DARVIN, AND LETTERS FROM PROMINENT
BALTIMOREANS IN TRIBUTE TO MANO SWARTZ

Presenting this pamphlet,
I wish it to be known
Every line is borrowed,
Not a word my own . . .

1940
PRIVATELY PRINTED

NOTE ON PAINTING

The plate on the opposite page is made from a large painting by D. W. Stokes, one of the many prominent artists of Mr. Swartz's acquaintance. Mr. Stokes painted it from life during the year 1931 in Mr. Swartz's office at 122 West Franklin Street, Baltimore. There luncheon was had daily among the innumerable books, papers, paintings and prints, which cluttered every part of the spacious room, making the place resemble a museum rather than an office.

While scores of distinguished persons lunched regularly with Mr. Swartz, Mr. Stokes included those who were most frequent guests and closest friends. Reading from left to right, about the table, are: Heinrich Turk, Dr. Oscar S. Benson, Willem Wirtz, Mano Swartz and Emmanuel Wad. Standing with paper in his hand, Leonard Darvin, secretary; the bearded gentleman, seated, is a foreign rabbi, name unknown--one of the many who were constant callers--and at the doorway, Waldemar Dietrich.

L. D.

Made in the USA
Charleston, SC
12 August 2016